Contents

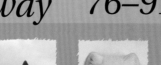

NORWAY

Geographical Location and Climate
Norway is the northernmost populated country in the world. With its location of approx. 58° at Lindesnes and 81° at the northern tip of Svalbard one would not believe it was possible for people to live here. If we compare other places between the same two latitudes, we find that the ice covered southern tip of Greenland lies at the same latitude as Oslo, and the magnetic north pole lies further south than Svalbard, at about the same latitude as Bjørnøya. Thanks to the Gulf Stream, which carries temperate water from the Gulf of Mexico, across the Atlantic Ocean, and up the whole of the Norwegian coast, the country has a climate that bears comparison with the climates of the other countries in Western Europe.

Population and Primary Industries
Following the last ice age the country was populated by primitive hunters and fishermen who made their homes in caves along the coast. Later on they learnt to cultivate the land. They built elegant ships for themselves that could cross the world's large seas. The Vikings are famous for their proud ships and ferocious journeys over the North Sea to England, the Baltic Sea to Estonia, Latvia, and Lithuania, south to Northern France, and all the way to Sicily where find traces of the Norsemen's culture can still be found in the large cathedrals.
The sea has thus always played a large role in the daily lives of Norwegians. It was the sea and the fjords that were the natural highways that bound them together, and thus Norway has always been amongst the world's leading maritime nations.
The large lowland areas of Jæren, in Eastern Norway and in Trøndelag were after a while put under the plough. Precious metals were found in the Norwegian mountains, and eventually industrial towns grew up in places where waterfalls provided reasonable waterpower for machines. Later on came electricity, which was very significant for industrial development, and nowadays modern technology has made it possible to drill for oil in the North Sea.

Historical Overview
Norway was united as one kingdom for the first time in 872 AD, and was an independent kingdom until 1397. Later on the country had a changeable history jointly sharing a king with Denmark and then one jointly with Sweden. From 1814 Norway has had its own constitution and from 1905 its own king, and its

6

own flag. The parliament is the country's lawmaking body. Norway's king is called Harald V.

Religion
Norway had its own primitive Norse mythology from prehistoric times until 1030 when King Olav the Holy forcibly imported Christianity. Today the Norwegian State Church belongs to the Lutheran Reformed Church, and the country has freedom of religion with a number of smaller religious communities.

Vegetation and Extent
As mentioned previously, Norway lies far to the north though the mild and humid prevailing southwesterly winds provide good conditions for people and plants. The country is self sufficient in most agricultural products, and forests that provide materials for house building and the pulp industry cover 1/4 of the land. In Southern Norway the forests grow up to altitudes of approx. 800 metres above sea level, and above the tree line the highest mountains rise up to over 2000 metres above sea level with Galdhøpiggen in Jotunheimen as the highest point at 2469 metres above sea level. Permanent snow lies on the highest mountains and in some places there are glaciers, remnants from the last ice age. The largest of them, the Jostedal glacier, is 74 km long and has an area of 480 km^2.
Norway is a long country stretching 1752 km from Lindesnes to the North Cape, though if we follow the coastline from the Swedish border in the south, to the Russian border in the north we have a 21,112 km journey to put behind us. Some 4.4 million people live in this 386,000 km^2 land.

Culture
The Vikings are famous for their ferocious, warlike journeys while it is less well known that they were also traders and important spreaders of culture in these northerly waters. The little that remains of their ships, domestic utensils, and jewellery bear witness to a highly developed culture, and we can see this was continued with the stave churches. In the last few centuries Norway has fostered famous cultural personalities such as the composers Ole Bull and Edvard Grieg, the writers Bjørnstjerne Bjørnson, Henrik Ibsen and Knut Hamsun, the polar researchers Fridtjof Nansen and Roald Amundsen, the artist Edvard Munch and the sculptor Gustav Vigeland,
In our time Thor Heyerdahl has kept the whole world excited with his voyages on the Kon-Tiki raft and the RA I and RA II reed boats.

Oslo

Oslo lies innermost in the Oslofjord, by the mouth of the river. The city has grown up out of a small trading place around the year 1048, though there was already a market place here in the Iron Age. Several fires ravaged the capital when at that time the city lay at the foot of the Ekeberg hill, and following the fire in 1624 King Christian IV decided that the city should be moved to the other bank of the River Aker, to the area around Akershus Castle. (Right) At that time it was called Christiania. The city got its university in 1811. The Royal Palace stood ready in the autumn of 1848. In 1925 the city took back its old name, Oslo. Oslo is now a city of around 500,000 inhabitants, it covers the whole of the area around the inner Oslo fjord, and is still famous for its beautiful surroundings, the seaside and its closeness to luxuriant forest and countryside. Despite being a city at the edge of Europe, Oslo has developed into a place with a continental variety of attractions for both tourists and its population.

Akershus Castle, which was built around the year 1300 AD. (Above)
The training ship, "Christian Radich", from Oslo. (Above)

The Royal Palace was rehabilitated in the 1990's at a cost of many millions, and is now the pride of the country and the people. (Left)

The parliament is situated in Oslo. The city's Town Hall is beautifully decorated. The National Theatre and The National Gallery are in the same centre, where the main street, Karl Johans gate, stretches between The Royal Palace and the main train station. On the West Side lies the Vigeland Park, containing the fantastic life's work of the sculptor Gustav Vigeland. The Norwegian Folk Museum is located on the Bygdøy peninsula. (Right) The Viking Ships House, The Fram Museum, The Kon-Tiki Museum, and The Norwegian Maritime Museum are also situated here.

(Left) "Two girls stand on their heads and laugh" and "Old man sitting and holding around 4 boys", from the circle of figures around the Monolith. (Right) "The Irascible" and "Man in a ring", both in bronze on the Bridge. The works of art in the park reflect the relationship between man and woman, the journey of life and our different moods. The artistic message from Gustav Vigeland itself is not specifically Norwegian, rather it is one that speaks volumes to tourists from all parts of the world.

The Vigeland Park covers an area of 320,000 m², and contains 212 sculptures in granite, bronze, and cast iron. The park has an 850 metre long main parade. The parade leads from the main entrance with its cast iron gates. The bridge with granite railings, 58 figures and groups in bronze, plus the children's place underneath next to the Frogner pond. Further on comes the Fountain that was the idea behind and start of the whole park. Several fantasy motifs with people and animals can be found here. The figures by the Fountain are not as powerful, and exhibit a carefully detailed naturalism. The Labyrinth, the square around the Fountain, covers an area of 1800 m² and is decorated with a mosaic in black and white granite. Three terraces higher up lies the Monolith Plateau and the Monolith. The granite column is carved out of a mountain block. Completely covered with 121 figures in high relief. Its total height and weight are 17,3 metres and approx. 180 tonnes. At the end of the parade stands the Wheel of Life. The Vigeland Park was entirely created by the sculptor Gustav Vigeland (1869-1943). The sculptures were produced between 1907 and 1942.

Holmenkollen Ski Jump, with its famous profile and faithful public. During the summertime concerts and competitions are arranged in the arena as well. Beneath the jump itself is the Ski Museum, with its rich collection of Norway's skiing and polar history. Close by is Holmenkollen Restaurant and, with a view over the city and the fjord, we find the exclusive Holmenkollen Park Hotel Rica. A Lapp from the exhibition at the Ski Museum. (Below)

Much of Norway's maritime history is gathered on Bygdøy. (Left) Fram, the ship specially built to withstand voyages in ocean regions with extreme cold and ice. She carried Fridtjof Nansen safely through the ice near the North Pole and Roald Amundsen to the ice's edge at the South Pole.

(Right) Kon-Tiki, Thor Heyerdahl's raft. The balsa wood raft that sailed across the Pacific Ocean from Peru to Polynesia, approx. 8000 km, in 1947.

(Below) Genuine Viking ship. It lay preserved in a burial mound for over 1000 years.

Eastern Norway

Eastern Norway has a coastline that stretches from Kragerø to the border with Sweden. This part of the country is less vulnerable to the weather and wind. Therefore we find large areas of cultivatable land here. In addition large tracts are covered by coniferous forest. The basis of the economy was hunting, fishing, agriculture, shipping, trade and later on industry. People first settled here after the ice age approx. 10,000 years ago. Visible signs of this are rock carvings found in several places. The towns have naturally grown up around the mouths of rivers. Each of the towns received privileges and a monopoly on trade. There has been significant export of timber goods from Eastern Norway to Holland, and the rest of Europe. The industrial cities of Sarpsborg and Fredrikstad lie on the banks of the river Glomma. On the other side of the fjord lies Tønsberg, which is Norway's oldest city, founded in the year 841 AD. The Mjøsa, Norway's largest lake, is situated in Eastern Norway. In the west there is also mountainous terrain.

Halden, below Fredriksten Fortress. (Above)

Moss, between Sweden and Oslo. (Left)

Fredrikstad, from the Old Town. (Right)

Svinesund, the Swedish - Norwegian border. (Below)

Gaustatoppen rises 1883 metres above sea level. From the top the mountain offers a panoramic view of the beautiful scenery of Telemark. At the top one can also see Hardangervidda, which is Europe's largest mountain plateau.

Rjukan. The industrial adventure of Norsk Hydro started here at the foot of the mountain where hydroelectric power was used to produce fertiliser.

Heddal is Norway's largest stave church. Raised around the year 1250 AD, the altarpiece is from the 1600's. The church was restored in the 1850's and is located at Notodden in Telemark.

Telemark - Haukeli and the mountain pass in June. (Above) Skien, (below left), with its 50,000 inhabitants is the centre of the county. The city lies on the banks of the River Skien, as does Porsgrunn. Buen cultural workshop, Tuddal. (Below). The barge "D/S Victoria" travels along the Telemark canal during the tourist season. (Next page).

The Southern Coast of Norway

The Southern Coast of Norway includes the skerries and the coast up to Flekkefjord, with an inland region. Kristiansand is the largest city with over 70,000 inhabitants. A city especially known for its ordered city architecture. Inherited from the founder, king Christian IV. While the other charming small towns lie, like a string of white pearls, where they grew up. In the centre we find the beautiful houses of merchants, ship owners, shipmasters, and pilots. Surrounding these lie the humble, but often well-kept ordinary inhabitants' homes. In the days of sail there was solid economic growth along the southern coast of Norway. Besides which, ships from all parts of Europe called at the coast's safe harbours. Therefore, piloting foreign ships into port became an important local trade. The basis of life was often a combination of fishing and agriculture. Tourism is now a very important source of income. In many of the small ports with boathouses there remains something in the air of the past's southern coast idyll and calmness. During the summer Norwegians from the whole of Eastern Norway are drawn here. As many as possible spend their holidays and weekends at their summer cottage.

(Below) Feda in the Fedafjord between Lista and Flekkefjord.

(Above) Flekkefjord in West-Agder

Lindesnes

2518 Nordkapp

(Left) Lindesnes lighthouse. The southernmost point in Norway.

(Below) Lillesand in Aust-Agder.

Tvedestrand, (left), is in many ways a typical small town amongst those to be found on the coast. Built around the harbour: with narrow streets and wooden houses. All protected from the wind and weather by a sheltered natural harbour.

Sjøsanden, (right), lies just next to Mandal. One of several popular beaches people seek out when the summer temperatures begin to rise. Sun, summer and bathing are therefore what many people associate this part of the country with.

Kristiansand (above and left), holidaymakers arrive from the skerries at the guest dock when they have an errand in the city. Merchants have lots of experience of serving summer tourists. The eastern harbour also has an airy and green park facing the sea.

(Next page) Blindleia - stretch of coast between Lillesand and Kristiansand.

Risør, East-Agder. The town is known for its annual wooden boat festivals, which attract more than 25,000 guests. The towns own population is 7,000. A well-maintained rescue vessel of the "Colin Archer" type. (Below) A vessel for the sea's toughest weather conditions. Designed by Colin Archer, who also designed the polar ship "Fram" for Nansen.

(Right) Arendal, East-Agder. Looking at Tyholmen with the Town Hall. The tall wooden house was originally built as the Kallvig yard in 1815. Ship building and shipyard business was carried out here in great style in the 1800's. Arendal is now thought of as one of the coast's pearls. With the guest harbour full of summer tourists. The town museum is also located at Tyholmen.

Grimstad, East-Agder. From the harbour, with typical white south coast wooden houses. These were the homes of ship owners, shipmasters, and others with high incomes and status. The town has an annual Ibsen festival. Henrik Ibsen (1828-1906), the writer, worked as a chemist's apprentice in the town between 1844 and 1850. (Below) Lyngør, East-Agder. A summer Eldorado on the skerries furthermost out towards the sea.

Western Norway

The part of the country from Flekkefjord to Kristiansund in the north, offers very varied scenery. In the south lies Jæren and typical lowland plains, covered by fields and meadows. Further north the landscape becomes wilder, with many deep fjords, and waterfalls plunging down steep mountainsides. There are also glaciers in some places. It was the power of these glaciers plus time that gave the fjords their characteristic U-shape. The basis of the economy was the traditional Norwegian one; characterised by the sea and unproductive soil. Bergen has been the most important trading place, while Stavanger has grown in step with the development of oil extraction in the North Sea. The northwestern region has a highly modern shipyard industry and fishing fleet. Tourism is of course also a very important part of the region's economic foundation, especially in the charming small communities we find in the fjords. It is without a doubt exactly these fjords that many outsiders associate with Norway.

(Above) "The Pulpit" in the Lysefjord in Rogaland - with a 604 metres drop to the sea.

(Right) Helleren in Jøssingfjord in Rogaland. There has been a settlement here since the 1600's.

(Previous page) Gudvangen at the bottom of the Nærøyfjord, Sogn and Fjordane.

(Above) Stavanger, Skagenkaien. The city's history goes back to Viking times. In the days of sail the city blossomed to the full. It has its own maritime museum. In the city itself there now live 100,000 inhabitants. With the oil adventure came many foreign companies too and Stavanger and its surrounding areas therefore have a pretty international population. Cruises along the Lysefjord to "The Pulpit" leave from Stavanger.

(Left) Old Stavanger. Old buildings in Stavanger have also been preserved for posterity, so that today we can enjoy the warm sheltered atmosphere one feels in this environment.

(Above) Gullfaks C - (Left) Draugen - the name comes from Norse mythology.

The first test drilling for oil and gas in the Norwegian continental field started in the 1960's. The first commercially exploitable finds were made in 1969 in the present day Ekofisk field. Statoil now operates the most comprehensive seafloor pipe system for the transport of gas. Direct to Europe or via Kollsnes in Øygarden west of Bergen. Kollsnes exports to France, the Netherlands, Belgium, Germany, the Czech Republic, Austria and Spain. The crude oil pipe system to the mainland ends at two terminals in Great Britain and at Mongstad and Sture in Hordaland. Tankers also load up from buoys in the North Sea. In 1997 the industry employed 22,000 people, and made up 176 billion crowns of the Gross National Product.

(Directly above) Låtefoss, near Odda in Hordaland.

(Above right) Sørfjorden, a branch of the Hardangerfjord, Hordaland.

(Left) Måbødalen, and State Road no. 7. The road to Vøringsfossen and Hardangervidda.

(Bottom right) Kjeaasen, the Simadals fjord. People have lived here since the 1300's. First road built in 1974. Before this, the fjord was the highway, and many a heavy load had to be hauled up the steep mountainside at the edge of Hardangervidda.

(Page 38-39) Steindalsfossen, Norheimsund on the Hardangerfjord.

(Top) Tvindefossen, with its many peculiar shelf like terraces, has a drop of approx. 150 metres. Next to the waterfall is Tvinde Camping, 12 km from Voss.

(Left) Stalheim Hotel, with Nærøydalen and Jordalsnuten in the background. The Stalheim Folk Museum, with its large collection of old farmhouses, is also situated in the traditional rich place.

(Above) The Aurlandfjord and Aurland with Flåm visible at the bottom of the Nærøyfjord. The fjord is just an arm of Sognefjord, Norway's longest, 200 km, and deepest, 1300 m.

(Right) Flåm, Sogn and Fjordane.

(Previous page) Borgund stave church in Sogn. The best preserved in Norway. Built in about 1200 AD, dedicated to St. Andreas, and later on neither rebuilt nor added to. Note the well-balanced proportions and the dragonheads on the gables.

(Above) Fjærland, Sogn and Fjordane. Tourist ships sail in here to admire the view. The fjord is coloured by melt water from the Bøya glacier. A part of the Jostedal glacier, North Europe's largest mainland glacier, approx. 480 km². The Norwegian Glacier Museum, a knowledge base about glaciers, ice, and snow, is located in Fjærland. Panoramic films of the Jostedal glacier, made by Ivo Caprino, are shown here.

(Right) The Bøya glacier, by the Fjærlandsfjord.

(Next page) The Briksdal glacier, Sogn and Fjordane. Among the most popular attractions in tourist Norway. On the right hand edge of the photo people are trekking over the ice.

(Left) From Briksdalbre Fjellstove horse drawn carts travel almost to the edge of the glacier. The local horses, "The Fjording", are well suited to the conditions, and ensure safe transport through the luxuriant, wild surroundings. Melt water from the glacier thunders down. The place has a long tradition as a tourist attraction. Different levels of glacier trekking are on offer.

(Below) Olden, Nordfjord. From here the first tourists travelled over Oldevatnet by boat and then inland by horse drawn transport to Briksdalbre Fjellstove. The motif also shows Oldvika with some of the manifold tourist ships that have visited the place.

Geiranger, in Møre and Rømsdal. The journey from the sea to Geiranger starts at Ålesund and the Storfjord. Along the way the fjord bends as if the steep mountain will halt the journey, but then the waterway opens up again and new impressions stream in.

The Geirangerfjord with waterfall. "The Seven Sisters". (Small photo)

(Next page) View of Trollstigen with "The Bishop" and "The King" peaks, in Møre and Romsdal.

Ålesund, Møre and Romsdal, The Jugend city in Western Norway. In 1904 a city wide fire raged through the old wooden buildings, leaving the city a pile of ashes. Like the phoenix bird the city rose again in the then modern Jugend style during 1904-1907. Almost 38,000 people live in this busy coastal city. The aerial photo shows the city on its islands.

(Left) Molde, Møre and Romsdal. The city of roses, with an annual Jazz festival.

Three islands form Kristiansund, (Right), and the city in connected by bridges and a lively harbour in the centre. Kristiansund is an intimate and exciting city while the Atlantic Ocean, its nearest neighbour to the west, forms a powerful contrast. The city is the dried cod capital of Norway and a tradition rich exporter. Nobody leaves Kristiansund without tasting "Bacalao" at one of the city's restaurants.

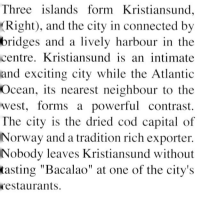

Bergen

Bergen is known for is beautiful location in the shelter of seven mountains and for its characteristic buildings. The city is supposed to have been founded by Olav Kyrre in 1070, but may be even older. It was not before the 19th century that Oslo overtook it as far as size goes, and today the city has 225,000 inhabitants. Bergen has a number of important sights of which we can mention; Bergenhus Castle, Mariakirken, Schøtstuene, Bryggen and Gamle Bergen Museum, all with reminders of Bergen's rich past. The city is also known for its modern aquarium. Bergen has several art galleries with both older and modern art, and in the region we can also find the Fantoft stave church, Lysekloster ruins, and Edvard Grieg's home, Troldhaugen.

The photo below shows Bryggen with buildings that are named on UNESCO's list of our common cultural heritage.

A natural part of a visit to Bergen is a trip on the Fløibanen which carries you 320 metres up from the city and offers the fines of panoramic views of the whole city and its surroundings, and out across the sea to the west. (Next page)

(Above) The Aquarium is located on Nordnes and, among other things, holds Europe's largest collection of saltwater fish and simpler sea animals.

Troldhaugen (below) was Nina and Edvard Grieg's home. It is built in the Victorian style, and lies next to Nordåsvannet, 8 km south of central Bergen. It is open to the public during the summer months.

The market (above) bulges with fresh goods, but the most famous are the tanks of live fish where the customers themselves can point out exactly the fish they want.
(Below right) the Rosenkrantz tower (built 1562-1568) looms large over the milieu around Vågen.
Håkonshallen (below left) was raised between 1248 and 1261 and restored in 1880-95 and 1958-61. Today it is the most distinguished of premises for large celebrations.

Mid Norway

The counties of Hedmark, Oppland, Trøndelag and the high mountains of southern Norway belong to this region. Sweden borders the area to east. The landscape along the national border is characterised by forests, marshes, and lakes. Otherwise large areas are above the tree line, and relatively few people live in the region. Industry and settlements are found in the valleys. Gudbrandsdalen, Norway's longest valley, is pretty typical. In southern Gudbrandsdalen, where mountains change to the Mjøsa region's gentle scenery, lies Lillehammer with approx. 25,000 inhabitants. The city was host to the 1994 Winter Olympic Games.

(Below) Glacier trekking on the Leir glacier at Krossbu, Lom in Oppland.

During the winter season there are lots of places for tourists to choose between. From Hafjell in the south to Oppdal in the north. The national parks are worth a visit during the summer and autumn. Rondane, Ormtjernkampen, Jotunheimen, Gutulia, Femundsmarka, and Dovre national parks are located here.

(Right) Musk Ox at Dovrefjell, Oppland. Attempts have been made to reintroduce the Musk Ox into the fauna of Norway. The previous herd was wiped out during the war. Today's herd comes from Greenland and was introduced to Dovre in the 50's.

(Above) Sognefjell, on the border between Sogn and Fjordane and Oppland.

(Above) Lillehammer, Oppland. A lovely city on the Mjøsa, which will long be remembered for the special atmosphere around the Winter Games in 1994. (Left) Maihaugen, De Sandvigske Samlinger in the city offers a unique insight into the local history, with about 150 culturally historic buildings in the open-air museum, founded in 1887.

(Right) "Skibladner" - The world's oldest paddle steamer. In operation on the Mjøsa since 1854.

Lysegårdbakkene - Olympic Games Arena, site of the opening ceremony.

(Above) Beito in Valdres facing Bitihorn, 1,608 metres above sea level.

(Left) The ski resort at Beitostølen starts in the centre and stretches up to 1,100 metres above sea level at Søndre Knaus-Høgdi. The season lasts from mid November until April.

(Above) Valdres Folk Museum, Fagernes. Year round regional open-air museum. The museum includes a hall with a national dress exhibition that encompasses the whole country. Daily folk music and dancing during the high season. Museum shop that sells among other things Norwegian handcrafts and folk music.

(Below) Bang in Valdres.

(Above) Glacier trekking towards Galdhøpiggen Northern Europe's highest mountain, 2469 metres above sea level.

(Left) Summer ski centre at the foot of Galdhøpiggen, 1850 metres above sea level. Modern ski resort with all facilities. The season lasts from June to mid November.

(Above) Along State Road no. 55 over Sognfjellet, approx. 40 km from Lom, lies Bøvertun, the oldest tourist area in the region. Guests have come to Bøvertun since 1864.

Rondane National Park , Norway's oldest, seen from Atnsjøen. There is a lot of tourist traffic along the well-marked paths, and many places to stay overnight. The summer season starts in the middle of June. During the spring special care must be taken due to the wild reindeers' calving. (Above) Turtagrø Hotel, Luster, on the road to Sognfjellet. (Top) Bjorli, Lesja in Gudbrandsdalen, and a swift river of melt water.

(Next page) Røros, Southern Trøndelag. The church tower and old buildings in Bergstaden.

Trondheim

Trondheim is known for is special location at the estuary of the idyllic River Nid. The city was supposedly founded by Olav Tryggvason in 997 AD. Building of the Nidarosdomen was started in the 1070's, (right) raised above the grave of Olav the Holy and when Norway got an archbishop, with Nidaros as his seat, in 1153 the city became the goal for pilgrims during large parts of the middle ages.

In addition to the national sanctum, the Nidarosdomen, Trondheim offers a number of sights. We might mention Erkebispegården, Hospitalkirken, the ruins of Olavskirken and Gregoriuskirken, as well as the Kristiansen Castle. All with rich memories of Trondheim's past.

The city's wooden buildings have been ravaged by fire many times, the largest in 1681, but well-preserved parts from 1700 and 1800's can still be found.

Today, Trondheim has approx. 146,000 inhabitants and is known as Norway's city of knowledge, with a university, a polytechnic and a number of research institutes.

(Above) Panoramic view of Trondheim with the Kristiansen Castle in the foreground.

(Right) The Olav Tryggvason statue stands in the market square. Made by Wilhelm Rasmussen in 1917-21. The statue and the column, which together are 18 metres tall, form the centre of a gigantic sundial.

(Left) State Engineer Dahl built Trondheim's "Old City Bridge" which was finished in 1861. When the bridge was widened somewhat in the 1950's the gallows that held the lifting wires were preserved, and it is these that today are referred to by the name "Fortune's Portal".

Northern Norway

This part of the country consists of Nordland, Troms, and Finnmark. The inland region has an extreme climate during the winter season. It is almost a form of polar desert where only especially adapted life survives. Finnmarksvidda is such an area, where temperatures of -50° have been measured. Meanwhile conditions are more favourable along the long coast. This is due to the Gulf Stream's water masses from the south. So the majority of the 465,000 population lives by coast. The rock carvings at Skjomen in Nordland may be 6000 years old. Caves at Træna, below the Arctic Circle, were home to hunters in the Stone Age. Fishing and hunting still play an important role in the region, though more and more people are employed in the service industries. Tourism is a good source of income, and it has in a way found its natural place in the North Country's culture. The tourists now stay in fishing shacks in the fishing villages, and there are still rich opportunities for fishing here. Whale safaris are another attractive possibility. Very many people are also attracted by the wild scenery, which is emphasised by the special lighting here. The North Cape and Knivskjelodden are natural goals and turning points for many. Norway and Europe's most northerly mainland, the mountain plateau drops more than 300 metres straight down into the Barents Sea.

(Above) Killer whales hunt for fish in herds in a northern fjord. There are several other species of whale here too.

(Left) The fishing fleet sails out to the fishing fields with empty holds and bilge wells, under the midnight sun.

(Right) Nusfjord in Lofoten. One of many fishing villages in the island group. Norwegian and foreign tourists come here to experience the scenery and people.

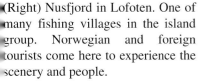

POLARCIRKEL
1937
19   40

The Arctic Circle, that famous invisible line, divides Norway at Svartisen National Park. This is where the midnight sun's realm begins, with nature's fascinating contrasts. Summer's light versus winter's darkness. Conditions that also have a positive effect on the population of the region.

(Right) The Arctic Circle Centre, at Saltfjellet, on the E6 highway.

(Above) The sea and skerries bathed in the midnight sun.

Svartisen, Norway's second largest glacier, with a surface area of 370 km², and thickness of 200 metres. The glacier is located in Saltfjellet - Svartisen National Park.

Hamnøy in Lofoten offers fantastic scenery, as well as activities for most people. Fishing cottage holidays with walking terrain, boat trips, fishing, diving, or simply the chance to just enjoy the life and the peace and quiet.

Lofotr, the Viking Museum at Borg. The chief's home was here in Lofoten ringed by smaller houses. (Above) The Viking ship "Lofotr" - a copy of the Gokstad ship from a burial mound in Vestfold, now in the museum at Bygdøy, Oslo. The building was also raised in the same historical style, something that creates an atmosphere and feeling of travelling 1000 years back in time. (Below)

Tromsø is the region's largest city with 58,000 inhabitants. Fishing and trade have been the main industries in the city. The coastal city is known colloquially as the "Paris of the North". Here too there is an almost continental nightlife and varied cultural activities. It has its own university and many museums. Tromsø is a coastal town spread over several islands. If one takes the mountain lift right to the top, (above) one is rewarded by a fabulous view.

(Previous page) Trollfjorden, Lofoten. When the weather gods permit it, both tourist ships and the coastal express, 'Hurtigruta', sail into the narrow fjord so passengers may experience the special atmosphere, which was possibly the inspiration for the name.

The North Cape and Knivskjelodden are located on Magerøya in Finnmark. With the inherent attraction of being Europe's northernmost point (71°11'08"N) the place has a magical drawing power on tourists. And the scenery itself ensures a worthy frame. The mountain plateau rises more than 300 metres above the Barents Sea, and serves as a brilliant viewing point.

The cliff formation has for centuries also functioned as a well-known navigation landmark for seafarers. Nowadays, the tourists have taken over, and a number of attractions now exist. The North Cape Hall houses a restaurant, bar, cafeteria, post office, and a large souvenir shop. Should conditions not be at their best, the Supervideograph, featuring a film by Ivo Caprino on a 225 degree screen, is an alternative. Magerøya is connected to the mainland via a tunnel.

(Below) "Kirkeporten" at Nordkapp

(Next page) A summer night at the Nordkapp.

(Above) Grazing reindeer. Each animal digs down to the plants under the snow.
(Below) Norway's national border with Russia stretches for over 196 km. Here in the north there has traditionally been pretty comprehensive trading between the neighbouring countries, and following the East's period of communism traffic and trade has increased.

The Lapps, who are reckoned to be Scandinavia's aboriginal people, live around Nordkalotten and some follow the reindeer herds as nomads living in tents. These people keep the traditional lifestyle alive. The colourful Lapp outfits are characteristic, which besides being a work of art, are functional in the extreme weather conditions the region exhibits. At least as many have been assimilated with the Norwegian population and live spread out across the whole country. (Above) A typical reindeer-drawn sledge. Note the broad hooves that carry the animal over the snow. There are also reindeer further inland to the south, on Hardangervidda, and in Rondane. In addition a separate herd of reindeer live on Svalbard.

(Right) Even tough nuts appreciate a little extra.

Svalbard

We are talking here about an island group far to the north with 62,700 km² of land. The first people here fished and hunted. Later on there were, and to a lesser degree still are, mining operations. Quite a bit of research is carried out on Svalbard. For a long time the islands were almost free of tourists due to transport, provisions, and the living situation. Svalbard's centre today is Longyearbyen. Much untouched, exciting scenery awaits tourists on Svalbard. Even though the summers are short, the days are long when the midnight sun hangs in the sky night and day. There is a fantastic amount of bird life here, as well as seals, walrus and whales in the sea, while on land liver arctic foxes and reindeer. And not forgetting that we find ourselves in the polar bear's realm. The giant which lives in the vast expanses of the ice desert. The scenery of Svalbard is also enormous, with black mountains and white surfaces. Glaciers cover over 50% of the landscape. Under special atmospheric conditions nature's own fireworks, the Northern Lights, appear in the sky.

(Below and next page) Longyearbyen.

The safety of the tourists has a high priority among those who arrange arctic safaris on Svalbard. This teddy bear is as cunning as it is big.

(Left) Arctic Fox. This white furred charmer survives in the extreme climate, but has also had to tolerate intense hunting for its fine coat. It is now protected by the closed season regulations of Svalbard, though still hunted during the winter.

(Below) The ice creates the most fantastic formations that can look like the most perfect of ice castles.

(Next page) The Northern Lights (Aurora Borealis) and stars. The phenomenon is caused by solar winds passing through the atmosphere at the Magnetic North Pole. Particles hit elements at high speed. The colour depends on the element that is hit. Duration 5-10 minutes.

The publication of "Norway" is the result of a partnership
between
Normanns Kunstforlag and To-Foto AS

Text:
Inge Stikholmen and Tom Granerud

Photography:
Trygve Gulbrandsen: pages 9 (top), 10-11, 18, 19 (top and bottom left),
24-31, 33 (top), 60 (top), 79 (top). Espen Bratlie: pages 20, 46, 59 (top).
Trond Tandberg: pages 1, 6-7, 32, 36-39, 40 (top), 43 (bottom), 48-49, 58, 66, 67 (top), 69.
Giulio Bolognesi: pages 8, 41 (bottom), 43 (top), 44 (bottom), 50 (bottom), 51 (bottom), 59 (bottom), 68, 70-73,
74 (bottom left), 75 (right), 79 (top). Per Andersen: pages 15 (bottom), 16. Mittet Foto: pages 17 (bottom), 34.
Dino Sassi: pages 9 (bottom), 10-11, 18, 19 (top and bottom left), 62-63, 65 (top), 67 (bottom).
Fjellanger Widerøe AS: pages 12-13, 19 (bottom right), 35, 41 (top), 50 (top), 51 (top), 54-55, 61 (top),
65 (bottom), 74 (top and bottom right), 80-81. Arne Normann: pages 2-3, 21 (bottom), 40 (bottom), 47,
60 (top), 64 (top). Willy Haraldsen: pages 42, 52, 53, 56, 57 (top and bottom right).
To-Foto AS: pages 76-78, 79 (bottom), 82-91. Siro Leonardi: pages 14, 17 (top).
Inge Stikholmen: page 64 (bottom). Herbert Czoschke: page 15 (top).
Odd Ivar Ruud: pages 92-96. Arvid Tjøsheim: page 33 (top).

Front cover photograph: NK/Giulio Bolognesi
Back cover photographs: Trond Tandberg, Willy Haraldsen,
Dino Sassi, Arne Normann, To-Foto AS.

Design: Haslum Grafisk AS
Pre-print: Haslum Grafisk AS
Printing: Haslum Grafisk AS

© NORMANNS KUNSTFORLAG

ISBN 82-7670-069-1
Art. No. 100/251